Addition in Word Problems

Some words often mean **to add.** Such words are called clue words. Some clue words that often mean to add are **total, sum, in all,** and **altogether.** Don't always expect to find clue words, so read the problems carefully.

Example: Henry's Hamburger Shop sold 227 hamburgers on Monday. On Tuesday 349 were sold. What was the total sold on the 2 days?

The Steps:
1. Read the problem carefully.
2. Look for possible word clues.
3. Decide what you must do.
4. Solve the problem.

The Problem: 227
             + 349
             ─────
              576

The Answer: A total of 576 hamburgers were sold.

Read and solve each problem.

1. French fries are sold in 2 sizes, regular and large. One week 487 regular and 754 large were sold. How many in all were sold that week?

   The Problem:

   The Answer: _____

2. Milly lives 17 blocks from Henry's Hamburger Shop. Bob lives 14 blocks away and Amy lives 6 blocks away. How many blocks must the 3 walk altogether to meet at Henry's?

   The Problem:

   The Answer: _____

3. A large cola costs 59¢. A small orange costs 39¢. If you buy 1 of each drink, what is the sum you owe?

   The Problem:

   The Answer: _____

4. Two days ago, 1,321 people were served at Henry's. Yesterday 1,899 were served. How many people were served on the 2 days?

   The Problem:

   The Answer: _____

Subtraction in Word Problems

Some words often mean **to subtract.** Here are some clue words that often mean subtraction is needed: **how many less, how many more,** and **difference.** Don't always expect to find clue words, so read the problems carefully.

Example: There are 11 players on a soccer team. A basketball team has 5 players. How many fewer players are on a basketball team?

The Steps:
1. Read the problem carefully.
2. Look for possible clue words.
3. Decide what you must do.
4. Solve the problem.

The Problem:
11
− 5
‾‾
6

The Answer: There are 6 fewer players on a basketball team.

Read and solve each problem.

1. Thirty-three girls went out for the school softball team last year. This year 41 went out. How many more went out this year?

   The Problem:

   The Answer: _____

2. The circumference of a baseball is about 23 cm. A basketball has a circumference of about 76 cm. What is the difference between the 2 in centimeters?

   The Problem:

   The Answer: _____

3. A major league baseball team bought 523 dozen baseballs at the beginning of the season. At the end of the season 97 dozen were left. How many dozen were used?

   The Problem:

   The Answer: _____

4. At one football game there were 12,468 fans. At the second game there were 39,865 fans. How many more were at the second game?

   The Problem:

   The Answer: _____

Addition or Subtraction in Word Problems

The Steps:
1. Read the problem carefully.
2. Look for possible word clues.
3. Decide what you must do.
4. Solve the problem.

Work the problems on another sheet of paper. Put your answers on this page.

1. There are 576 pupils in Winthrop School. At the M.L. King School there are 645 pupils. How many more pupils are at M.L. King?

   _____

2. If there are 576 pupils at Winthrop and 645 at M.L. King, how many pupils are there in all?

   _____

3. There are 301 girls at M.L. King School. Winthrop School has only 284. What is the total number of girls in the 2 schools?

   _____

4. On Wednesday 23 pupils were absent from Winthrop School. On Thursday 36 were absent, and on Friday 17 pupils were out. What was the total number of students absent for the 3 days? _____

5. M.L. King School has 645 pupils. Of those students, 301 are girls. How many are boys?

   _____

6. Of the 576 pupils who go to Winthrop School, 87 walk. The others ride buses. How many more pupils ride buses than walk to Winthrop School?

   _____

7. Last year 595 pupils attended Winthrop School. This year the attendance is 576. What's the difference in the attendance between the 2 years?

   _____

8. The M.L. King School cafeteria seats 214 pupils. The Winthrop cafeteria is much smaller. It seats only 127 pupils. How many fewer can be seated in the cafeteria at Winthrop than at M.L. King? _____

Multiplication in Word Problems - 1

When doing word problems, remember to read carefully. Look for word clues that will help you decide what to do.

Example: Alfred owns a big dog named Binky. Binky eats 2 cans of dog food every day. How many cans would be needed to feed Binky for 30 days?

The Steps:
1. Read the problem carefully.
2. Look for possible word clues.
3. Decide what you must do.
4. Solve the problem.

The Problem: 30
                   x 2
                   ———
                   60

The Answer: 60 cans would be needed.

Read and solve each problem.

---

1. Cat food is on sale. You can buy 3 cans for $1.00. If you bought $6.00 worth, how many cans would you buy?

   The Problem:

   The Answer: _____

---

2. The largest and heaviest animal is the blue whale. A 100-foot blue whale weighs about 179 tons. How many tons would 15 of them weigh?

   The Problem:

   The Answer: _____

---

3. The egg of the whale shark can be 30 cm long. Suppose you place 49 such eggs end to end. How many centimeters long would that line of whale shark eggs be?

   The Problem:

   The Answer: _____

---

4. The fastest that one kind of turtle can move is about 5 yards in 1 minute. How many yards could it move in 15 minutes?

   The Problem:

   The Answer: _____

Multiplication in Word Problems - II

The Steps:
1. Read the problem carefully.
2. Look for possible word clues.
3. Decide what you must do.
4. Solve the problem.

Work the problems on another sheet of paper. Put your answers on this page.

1. Paul's parents have an old car. The car gets 18 miles to a gallon of gasoline. How many miles can the car travel on 15 gallons?

   _____

2. Rae's parents have a new car. Their car gets 27 miles to a gallon of gas in town driving. On the highway it gets 42 miles to a gallon. How many miles can it go on 8 gallons if the car is driven only in town?

   _____

3. One automobile factory turns out 780 cars a day. If the month of December has 21 working days, how many cars will be turned out that month?

   _____

4. A car dealer has 14 new cars to sell. Each car sells for $5,299. If the dealer sold all the cars, how much money would the dealer take in?

   _____

5. Sam's dad runs a service station. He sells about 18 new tires each week. About how many tires would he sell over a period of 52 weeks?

   _____

6. Gasoline was cheaper in 1950 than it is now. One gas station sold its gas for 20¢ a gallon. For just $1.00 you could get 5 gallons. If the station sold $55 worth of gas one day, how many gallons were sold?

   _____

7. Terri's mom uses her car for business. She drives about 1,800 miles a month. About how many miles would Terri's mom cover in 1 year of driving?

   _____

School Zone Publishing Co.

Division in Word Problems - 1

When doing word problems, remember to read carefully. Look for word clues that will help you decide what to do.

Example: A supermarket sold 640 boxes of cereal in 5 days. If about the same amount were sold each day, about how many would be sold on each of the days?

The Steps:
1. Read the problem carefully.
2. Look for possible clues.
3. Decide what you must do.
4. Solve the problem.

The Problem:

```
      128
   5)640
     -5
     ---
     14
    -10
    ---
     40
    -40
    ---
      0
```

The Answer: 128 boxes each day.

Read and solve each problem.

1. There are 132 pieces of candy in a bag. The pieces are to be shared equally between 6 people. How many pieces will each person get?

   The Problem:

   The Answer: _____

2. A chicken farmer collects 648 eggs one morning. He packs them 12 to a carton. How many cartons would the eggs fill?

   The Problem:

   The Answer: _____

3. A chocolate chip cookie bakery turns out 636 cookies an hour. How many dozen cookies would that be?

   The Problem:

   The Answer: _____

4. Suppose a bag contains 42 apples to be divided equally between 7 people. How many apples would each person receive?

   The Problem:

   The Answer: _____

Division in Word Problems - II

What happens if a division problem comes out with a remainder?

Example: A bag of 1,001 marbles is to be divided between 24 persons. How many marbles does each person get?

The Steps:
1. Read the problem carefully.
2. Look for possible word clues.
3. Decide what you must do.
4. Solve the problem.

The Problem:

```
      41R17
24|1001
    96
    ―――
     41
     24
    ―――
     17
```

The Answer: Each person gets 41, and there is a remainder of 17.

Work the problems on another sheet of paper. Put your answers on this page. Not all problems have remainders.

1. A store has 126 bags of marbles for sale. Suppose 6 bags are sold each day. How many days will it take to sell all the marbles?

   _____

2. Fourteen persons are playing marbles. Between the persons there are a total of 879 marbles. About how many marbles does each person have?

   _____

3. A marble machine can make 128,000 marbles in an hour. If those marbles are packed into 25 cartons, how many marbles will be in each carton?

   _____

4. You want to divide a box of marbles into as many groups of 28 as you can. If there are 1,209 marbles in the box, what will the result be?

   _____

5. Suppose 1 pupil out of 5 in a school has some marbles. If the school has 675 pupils, how many own marbles?

   _____

6. A marble machine turns out equal amounts of 3 different colors of marbles. If 33,000 marbles are turned out, how many are there of each color?

   _____

School Zone Publishing Co.

Addition? Subtraction? Multiplication? Division? - 1

The Steps:
1. Read the problem carefully.
2. Look for possible word clues.
3. Decide what you must do.
4. Solve the problem.

Work the problems on another sheet of paper. Put your answers on this page.

1. Nan has a newspaper route. She delivers 56 papers each day. She delivers the papers 6 days a week. How many newspapers does she deliver in a week?

   _____

2. Ned also has a paper route. He delivers 294 papers in all. If he works 6 days, what is the number he delivers each day?

   _____

3. During 1 week Nan collected $112, not including tips. Since she delivered papers to 56 customers, how much does each customer pay for the paper?

   _____

4. One week Ned earned 75¢ more in tips than Nan. If Ned took in $12.75 in tips, how much did Nan make in tips that week?

   _____

5. Both Nan and Ned deliver their papers after school. Nan starts her route at 4:30. Ned doesn't start until 15 minutes later. At what time does Ned start?

   _____

6. Nan needs to save $36 to buy presents. She puts aside $6 a week from the money she makes from her paper route. How many weeks will it take for her to save the $36?

   _____

7. Sometimes Ned's brother Bert delivers Ned's papers. Out of 304 days in one year, Bert delivered on 17 of the days. How many days out of the 304 did Ned do the delivery?

   _____

8. Ned kept his route for 3 years. Then his brother Bert delivered the paper for 4 years. Nan kept her route for 5 years. How many more years did Nan deliver papers than Ned?

   _____

Addition? Subtraction? Multiplication? Division? - II

The Steps:
1. Read the problem carefully.
2. Look for possible word clues.
3. Decide what you must do.
4. Solve the problem.

Work the problems on another sheet of paper. Put your answers on this page.

1. According to one survey most sixth grade pupils watch TV about 3 hours a day. How many hours a week would that be?

   _____

2. American kids watch about 25,000 television commercials in a year. About how many commercials would that be for each month of the year?

   _____

3. Most American high school graduates are 18 years old. By that time they will have watched about 15,000 hours of television. About how many hours will 17 high school graduates have watched?

   _____

4. A store has 97 black-and-white television sets on sale. If all but 14 are sold, how many were sold?

   _____

5. In the homes on Elm Street, there are 37 TV sets. On Maple Avenue there are 48 sets. And on Beech Drive there are 28 sets. How many TV sets in all are there in the homes?

   _____

6. On High Street there are 49 homes having 2 or more TV sets. At least how many TV sets are in those 49 homes?

   _____

7. In 1 home the TV is on about 42 hours a week. In another home the TV is on about 24 hours a week. What's the difference in viewing hours in the 2 homes?

   _____

Problems With More Than One Math Step

In some word problems you will need to do only one math step. In others you may have to do more than one math step.

Example: There were 69 library books taken out on Monday. Alice checked out 6 books. Boris checked out 3 books. How many books were checked out by other persons?

Math Step 1 (addition) 6 + 3 = 9

Math Step 2 (subtraction) 69 - 9 = 60

Answer: There were 60 books checked out by other persons.

Work the problems on another sheet of paper. Put your answers on this page.

1. Three times as many library books were checked out on Tuesday as on Wednesday when 37 were checked out. How many books were checked out on the 2 days?

   _____

2. The librarian bought a set of new encyclopedias for the library. The set cost $750. There were 25 books in the set. How much did it cost for each group of 5 books?

   _____

3. Cindy wanted to buy 3 books in a bookstore. The first one was $2, the second $5, and the third $4. The cost for each included the tax. Cindy handed the sales clerk $15. How much change did Cindy receive back?

   _____

4. Dan bought 2 comic books at a used book sale. The comic books were selling 6 for 90¢. How much did Dan pay for the 2 comic books that he had picked out?

   _____

5. The library has 107 new mysteries and 29 new sports books. They were added to the 206 mysteries and 117 sports books already in the library. How many more mysteries than sports books does the library now have?

   _____

Averages - 1

How do you find the average of a set of numbers? First you add the numbers, then you divide the sum by the number of members in the set.

Example: On Monday 3 persons were absent from a class. On Tuesday 1 person was absent. On the other 3 days that week, 4, 4, and 3 persons were absent. What was the average number absent?

Average Step #1
(add the absences)

```
  3
  1
  4
  4
  3
 ──
 15
```

Average Step #2
(Divide the sum by the number of days.) $15 \div 5 = 3$

Absences
Eddie Karat
Fanny Jones
Ginger Dim

Work the problems on another sheet of paper. Put your answers on this page.

1. There were 3 lunch periods in Brookwood School. The first period 137 persons were served. In the second and third periods, 141 and 169 persons were served. What was the average number of persons served during a lunch period at Brookwood School?

   _____

2. Eddie walks to school. He wants to find the average amount of time it takes him to walk. He kept track of his time for 6 days. The times in minutes were 12, 10, 13, 12, 11, and 14. What is the average number of minutes it takes Eddie to walk to school?

   _____

3. Fanny rides the school bus. One day she waited 7 minutes for the bus. On some other days she waited 5, 9, 8, and 6 minutes. What was the average wait of these days?

   _____

4. Ginger has 5 pencils. Harry has 4. Ida has 6, and Jack has 12. Karla has 7, and Lenny only has 2. What is the average number of pencils owned by all the persons listed?

   _____

5. Maureen uses 6 textbooks. They have different amounts of pages. They are 348, 336, 228, 296, 96, and 124. What is the average amount of pages in the textbooks she uses?

   _____

Averages - II

Do the four **Word Problem Steps:**

1. Read the problem carefully.
2. Look for possible word clues.
3. Decide what you must do.
4. Solve the problem.

Then do the **Finding Averages Steps:**

1. Add the numbers in a set.
2. Divide the sum by the number of members in the set.

Work the problems on another sheet of paper. Put your answers on this page.

1. Carla played in 4 softball games. In the first game she had 1 hit. She had 2 hits each in the second and third games. In the last game she had 3 hits. What was the average number of hits she had in the 4 games in which she played?

   _____

2. Ben played on a different team. In 11 games he got the following in hits: 3, 0, 1, 2, 0, 4, 3, 2, 1, 3, and 3. What was the average number of hits Ben made in those games?

   _____

3. The Lions and Tigers played a game. In the first 5 innings, the Lions scored 0, 1, 0, 2, and 0 runs when they were at bat. The Tigers scored 0, 2, 0, 0, and 5. What was the average number of runs scored in the 5 innings by the 2 teams?

   _____

4. There were 378 persons at the first game played between the Lions and Tigers. The 2 teams played 4 more games. At those games there were 216, 496, 389, and 421 persons. What was the average number of persons at each of the 5 games?

   _____

5. The Tigers play 25 games each year. Over a 6-year period they had the following number of wins: 14, 19, 18, 9, 13, and 23. What was their average number of wins those 6 years?

   _____

6. Each year the Lions get new baseball caps. Last year 27 caps were bought. This year the manager bought 25. Next year 29 will be needed. What is the average number of caps over the 3 years?

   _____

Fractions - Mixed Numbers - Addition and Subtraction

What's a mixed number? The combination of a whole number and a fraction, such as 2 ¼. To do a word problem with mixed numbers, do the four Word Problem steps. Then, in addition or subtraction problems, there are two **Mixed Number Steps** to do:

1. Add or subtract the fractional parts.
2. Add or subtract the whole number parts.

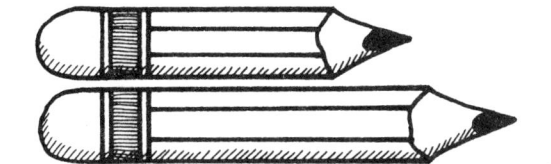

You may also need to do an additional step or two:

3. If the fraction denominators are not alike, change them to equivalent fractions.
4. Regroup the sum of the fractional parts if the sum is greater than or equal to one.
5. Reduce the fraction answer.

Work the problems on another sheet of paper. Put your answers on this page.

1. Mary's pencil is 14 2/5 cm long. Nancy's is 16 1/5 cm long. If the 2 pencils were placed end to end, how long would they now be?

   _____

2. Opie has a new pencil that is 7 2/5 inches long before being sharpened. Pearl's pencil is 5 1/5 inches long. What is the difference in length between the 2 pencils?

   _____

3. Reggie's pen weighs 2 1/3 ounces. Sandra's pen is somewhat heavier. Her pen weighs 3 1/2 ounces. If the 2 pens were weighed together, what would the combined weight be? _____

4. Theresa's pencil box weighs 1 3/4 pounds. Una's pencil box weighs 1 1/3 pounds. What's the difference in weight?

   _____

5. Vera's pencil box weighs 1 5/8 pounds. Willy's box weighs 1 3/8 pounds. What's the combined weight of the 2 boxes?

   _____

6. Xena's math book is 9 7/8 inches long. Her reading book is 7 3/4 inches long. What's the difference in length?

   _____

7. Zeke owns a ruler. It broke into two pieces. One piece was 7 5/8 inches long. The other piece was 4 3/8 inches long. If the two pieces were placed together, how long would they be? _____

Fractions - Mixed Numbers - Multiplication and Division

Do the four **Word Problem Steps:**
1. Read the problem carefully.
2. Look for possible word clues.
3. Decide what you must do.
4. Solve the problem.

There are two ways to multiply mixed numbers. Either change to fractions and multiply, or multiply just as you do whole numbers.

What's the easiest way to divide mixed numbers? Change them to fractions first. Remember to always give your fraction answers in lowest form.

Work the problems on another sheet of paper. Put your answers on this page.

1. Mark picked 2 boxes of apples. Each box has 3 1/2 dozen apples in it. How many apples in all did Mark pick?

   _____

2. Nina had an empty egg carton. It had room for 12 eggs. She filled it 5/6 full. How many eggs were in the carton after Nina filled it 5/6 full of eggs?

   _____

3. Pete wanted to find the answer to the following problem: 1 1/2 of 1 1/3. Pete did the problem carefully. He followed the four Word Problem Steps. Then he multiplied. He came out with the correct answer because he did the problem properly. What was his answer? _____

4. Rita needs to solve the following problem: 50 ÷ 1 1/2. If Rita does the problem correctly, what will her answer be?

   _____

5. You have a roll of tape that is 48 cm long. How many 5 1/3 cm long pieces can you cut from this roll of tape?

   _____

6. Here's a problem to which you can find the answer. Remember to do all the necessary steps: 4 1/2 ÷ 2 3/4.

   _____

Decimal Fractions - Addition and Subtraction

Do the four **Word Problem Steps.** The following special steps for adding and subtracting decimals also apply:

1. Set up the problem.
2. Line up the decimal points.

Example: Paula wants to find the sum of 19.3 and 6.45 in order to complete a test. If her answer is correct, what would it be?

$$\begin{array}{r} 19.3 \\ + 6.45 \\ \hline 25.75 \end{array}$$

Work the problems on another sheet of paper. Put your answers on this page.

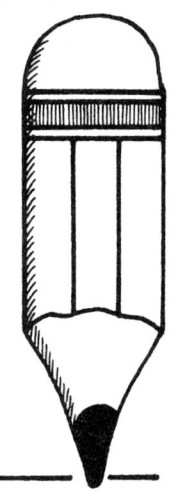

1. Rex grew 4.5 inches this year. Last year he grew 5.4 inches. How much did he grow in those 2 years?

   _____

2. Sandra is shorter than Tess. Tess is 165.4 cm tall. Sandra is only 150.2 cm tall. What is the difference in their height?

   _____

3. Vern bought 3 books. They cost $4.16, $2.95, and $6.50. How much money in all did Vern spend for the 3 books?

   _____

4. Wes started out the day with $14.83. He was going shopping to buy presents. At the end of the day Wes had spent $11.17. How much money did he have left?

   _____

5. Abbie wanted to find the difference between 14.654 and 456.418. Suppose you did the same problem as Abbie, and suppose the two of you came up with the same answer. What is it?

   _____

6. Bess has some strips of paper. The strips are 14.23, 7.17, 29.08, and 9.88 cm long. What is the total length of the 4 strips that Bess has?

   _____

7. Candy knows 8.71 is a lot less than 317.88 is. If she wants to find the difference, she subtracts one from the other. What does she find that difference to be?

   _____

Decimal Fractions - Multiplication and Division

Do the four **Word Problem Steps.** The following special steps for multiplying and dividing also apply.

For Multiplication
1. Set up the problem.
2. Count the number of digits to the right of each decimal point in the problem.
3. To place the decimal point in the answer, count off to the left, the same number of digits.

Example:
```
   9.99
 x  .9
  8.991
```

For Division
1. Line up decimal points in the dividend and quotient.
2. If divisor has a decimal point, move to the right. If dividend also has a decimal, move it the same number of digits to the right.

Example:

.7)77.77 = .7)77.77 quotient 111.1

Work the problems on another sheet of paper. Put your answers on this page.

1. Ken decided to buy 3 hamburgers. Each cost 59¢. What was the total Ken paid for the 3 hamburgers?

   _____

2. Lou finds it easy to multiply with decimals. She quickly found the answer when she multiplied .63 by 77.7. What was the answer?

   _____

3. Meridith weighs 79 pounds. On the moon she would weigh only about .17 as much. What would Meridith's weight be if she were to find herself on the moon?

   _____

4. Pam buys 7 pencils for $1.05. How much does each of the pencils cost if each costs the same amount?

   _____

5. Nancy wants to divide 8 into .888. If she does the problem correctly, what is the answer?

   _____

16   Multiplication or division of decimal fractions   02042

Assorted Problems

Do the four **Word Problem Steps:**
1. Read the problem carefully.
2. Look for possible word clues.
3. Decide what you must do.
4. Solve the problem.

These problems made me hungry!

Work the problems on another sheet of paper. Put your answers on this page.

1. Henry's Hamburger Shop had 2 busy days on Monday and Tuesday. On Monday $417.83 was taken in, and $597.37 was taken in on Tuesday. What was the total take for the 2 days?
   _____

2. The owner of Henry's found that only 1/6 as many root beers were sold as colas. One day 534 colas were sold. About how many root beers were sold on that day?
   _____

3. During 1 week 2,219 bags of French fries were sold. What was the average number sold each day in that week?
   _____

4. As a rule fewer strawberry milk shakes are sold than vanilla shakes. On 1 Friday 116 vanilla shakes were sold. The number of strawberry shakes sold was 67 fewer. How many were sold?
   _____

5. In 1921, hamburgers cost only 5¢. Suppose you had gone to buy hamburgers in 1921. How many would you get put into a bag if you had $1.00 to spend?
   _____

6. A large cheeseburger at Henry's costs $1.45. If you make one just like it at home the cost is only 80¢. If you made 2 cheeseburgers at home, how much would you save over the $2.90 you would have spent at Henry's for 2?
   _____

7. Henry's puts 3 pickle slices on each burger. If 2,961 pickle slices were used, how many burgers were prepared?
   _____

8. Henry's took in an average of $315.29 each day last year. How much money overall was taken in that year?
   _____

Percent - I

Problem: Dan answers 20 questions on a test. Of the answers, 17 were correct. What percent did Dan answer correctly?

Rule: When you are given the figures, but not the percent, you find the percent by dividing a larger number into the smaller.

Example:

```
        .85
    20 ⟌ 17.00
        160
        ---
        100
        100
        ---
          0
```

.85 = 85%

Things to Do:
1. Place a decimal point after the last digit in the dividend if you need to add zeros to divide.
2. Place the decimal in the quotient directly above the one in the dividend.
3. To change the decimal to a percent, move the decimal point 2 places to the right.

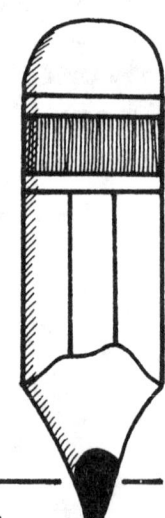

Work the problems on another sheet of paper. Put your answers on this page.

1. Dan's sister went to the bakery for a loaf of bread. At the bakery Darlene saw 60 loaves for sale. Of the loaves, 15 were rye bread. What percent of the loaves were rye?

2. The high school to which Dan will go had 720 graduates last year. Out of the 720, 360 went to college. What percent of the students went to college?

3. Dan's little brother had a birthday party. Forty balloons were bought for the party, and 32 were blown up. What percent of the balloons were blown up?

4. At Darlene's school 56 out of 280 sixth graders brought their lunch to school. What percent brought their lunch?

5. Darlene had a spelling test with 150 words. She spelled 120 of the words correctly. What was the percent answered correctly?

6. Dan's Little League started out with 2,400 candy bars to sell. At the end of the sale, 2,208 bars had been sold. What percent of the total had been sold?

18   Working percent word problems   02042   School Zone Publishing Co.

Percent - II

Problem: Edith earned $450 from her paper route last year. She saved 40% of the money. How much did she save?

Rule: When the percent is one of the numbers given, you multiply to get the answer.

Example:
```
    $450
  x  .40
    ----
     000
    1800
   ------
   $180.00
```

Things to Do:
1. Change the percent to a decimal fraction.
2. To change the percent to a decimal fraction, move the decimal point 2 places to the left.
3. If the percent has only 1 digit, add a zero to the left of it before adding the decimal point (Ex. 4% = .04).

Work the problems on another sheet of paper. Put your answers on this page.

1. Edith's mom planted 500 seeds in her vegetable garden. If 95% of the seeds sprouted, how many seeds would that be?

   _____

2. Edith received a beautiful transistor portable radio for her birthday. It cost $120, and there was a 5% tax charged also. How much was the tax?

   _____

3. Edith's brother, Fran, plays tennis. Fran went to a store to buy a new racket. The store had 225 for sale. Of the rackets, 36% were black and white in color. How many of them were black and white?

   _____

4. Edith's mom drives to work. She parks the car in a garage in the city. There are 740 parking spaces in the garage. Usually there are cars in 85% of the parking spaces. What number of cars usually park in the garage?

   _____

5. The rent for the apartment in which Edith lived was $160. If the rent increased 6%, how much would the increase be?

   _____

6. Edith's mom bought a new suit at a 15% savings. How much did she save if the original cost of the suit was $80?

   _____

School Zone Publishing Co.

Percent - III

Remember the two rules to look for when doing percent problems:

Rule 1. When you are given the figures, but not the percent, you find the percent by dividing the larger number into the smaller.

Rule 2. When the percent is one of the numbers given, you multiply to get the answer.

Work the problems on another sheet of paper. Put your answers on this page.

1. Bertha went shopping to buy some T-shirts. One store had 500 T-shirts for sale. Five of them were red in color. What percent of the T-shirts were red?

   _____

2. Boris was reading one of the books in a set of encyclopedias. If he has already read 30% of the 630 pages, how many pages in all has Boris read?

   _____

3. Bertha's dad works in the city. Of the 430,000 workers, 35% of them ride to work in cars. How many ride in cars?

   _____

4. The auditorium in Bertha's school has 600 seats. Of the seats, 72 were just repaired. What percent of the seats in the auditorium were repaired?

   _____

5. Out of the 365 days in the year, Boris worked 146. What percent of the whole year did he work?

   _____

6. Boris is left-handed. Of the 720 pupils in Brookwood School, 10% are left-handed. How many of the pupils are lefties?

   _____

7. Bertha had $145 in her savings account at the bank. If she withdrew 12% of it, how much money would she take out?

   _____

Percent - Mixed Numbers

Problem: On Monday 12 ½ % of the students in Brookwood School were absent. How many of the school's 600 pupils did not come in that day?

Example:
```
    600
  x .125
   3000
   1200
   600
  75.000
```

Things to Do:
1. Change the percent to a decimal fraction.
2. Change the fraction to one or more whole numbers (10 ¼ %, for example, would become .1025).

Work the problems on another sheet of paper. Put your answers on this page.

1. Karen plays on a basketball team. Karen is a good free throw shooter. She had 32 free throws last season, and she made 87 ½ % of them. How many free throws did she make?

    _____

2. In Karen's neighborhood 800 people own TV's. Of those people, 62 ½ % own color TV's. How many of the people in the neighborhood own color TV's?

    _____

3. Karen has a savings account that pays 6 ¼ % interest each year. If she leaves $124 in her account for one year, how much interest will she make?

    _____

4. Karen's parents have $10,000 invested in 15 ½ % interest. How much interest will the $10,000 draw in 1 year?

    _____

5. Karen wants to find what percent 8 is of 100. Kevin tells her to divide the smaller number by the larger number. If Karen does the problem correctly, what percent will she end up with?

    _____

6. Kevin then asks Karen to find what percent 5 is of 8? If Karen divides the smaller number by the larger number, what answer in percent does she get?

    _____

School Zone Publishing Co. 02042 Working mixed number percent word problems

Perimeter Word Problems

Rule 1. To find the perimeter of a figure, you add the lengths of its sides.

Rule 2. If two or more sides are equal, you can also use a multiplication step.

Rule 3. Make certain all units are the same before adding or multiplying.

Problem: Beth jogs around Center Park each afternoon. The park measures 300 meters on each of 2 sides, and 568 and 572 meters on the other 2 sides. How many meters in all will Beth travel if she goes around Center Park once?

Examples:

```
    300                    2 x 300 = 600
    300                              568
    568        or                  + 572
  + 572                            1740 meters
   1740 meters
```

Work the problems on another sheet of paper. Put your answers on this page.

1. Chris walked around a rectangular building. The building was 613 yards long and 389 yards wide. How far did Chris have to walk to get around the building?

   _____

2. Chris went inside the building. He found the counter where watches were sold. The counter was triangular in shape. To walk around the counter Chris traveled 37 meters. If the distance around 2 of the sides equaled 29 meters, what was the length of the third side? _____

3. Outside the building was a 6-sided sign. If each of the sides was 48 cm long, what was the perimeter of the sign?

   _____

4. Chris bought a poster for his room. The poster measured 18 ½ inches wide and 36 inches long. How many inches more than 100 was its perimeter?

   _____

5. Chris wanted to find what the perimeter of the top of his match book was in millimeters. He found the length to be 243 mm and the width to be 192 mm. What was the perimeter?

   _____

Area Word Problems

Rule 1. To find the area of a rectangle, you multiply the length by the width. Your answer will be in square units. Use the formula **A = l x w** to do problems.

Rule 2. To find the area of a triangle, **A = ½ x base x height** is the formula to use. Your answer will be in square units.

Rule 3. Make certain units are the same before you multiply.

Problem: Fritz is planting 2 flower beds. One is rectangular with a length of 3 meters and a width of 2 meters. The other flower bed is triangular. Its base is 4 meters and its height is 1.5 meters. What is the area of each of the flower beds?

Examples:

A = l x w
A = 3 m x 2 m
A = 6 square m

A = ½ x b x h
A = ½ x 4 m x 1.5 m
A = ½ x 6 square m
A = 3 square m

Work the problems on another sheet of paper. Put your answers on this page.

1. Juanita wants to get a new wall-to-wall rug for her room. If her room measures 12 x 16 feet, what's the area she needs to cover?

   _____

2. Juanita's brother broke a window pane in the kitchen. How many square centimeters of glass will he need to replace if the old pane had a length of 19 cm and a width of 17.5 cm? _____

3. The kitchen table measures 6 feet 6 inches by 3 feet. To completely cover the top, what would be the least area that would be needed for a tablecloth?

   _____

4. Juanita mows a neighbor's side yard in summer. She uses a power mower and it takes her 45 minutes. The side yard is rectangular in shape, measuring 77.6 meters by 49.3 meters. What's the area of the side yard Juanita mows each week? _____

5. Juanita mows a small triangular-shaped lawn in back of the neighbor's house with a hand mower. If that lawn's base is 7.3 m and its height is 3.8 m, what's the area of that lawn's triangle? _____

Volume Word Problems

Rule 1. To find the volume of a rectangular solid, you multiply its length times its width times its height. You use the formula **V = l x w x h** to find your answers.

Rule 2. Make certain all units are the same before multiplying.

Rule 3. Your answers will be in cubic units.

Problem: Ted's aquarium measures 50 cm by 20 cm by 25 cm. What is its volume in cubic centimeters?

Example:
V = l x w x h
V = 50 cm x 20 cm x 25 cm
V = 25,000 cubic centimeters

Work the problems on another sheet of paper. Put your answers on this page.

1. Sandra has a large aquarium in her room. Its dimensions are 70 cm by 30 cm by 36 cm. What's the volume of Sandra's aquarium?

   _____

2. Sandra knows that 1,000 cubic centimeters is equal to 1 liter. She knows the liter is 1 unit used for measuring liquid volume. She has a small aquarium that has a volume of 36,000 cubic cm. How many liters of water would the aquarium hold if filled to the top? _____

3. Sandra has an empty aquarium. The dimensions of the aquarium are 45 cm by 25 cm by 25 cm. If she fills the aquarium completely with sand, how much sand will she need?

   _____

4. Sandra wants to find out how much water it would take to fill the empty aquarium she owns. (See problem #3 for the aquarium dimensions.) How many liters of water would the aquarium hold?

   _____

5. An aquarium at school is 50 cm long and 18.8 cm wide. It is filled to a depth of 22 cm with water. How many cubic centimeters of water are in the aquarium? How many liters would that be?

   _____ cubic cm   _____ liters

24 Working word problems concerning volume 02042   School Zone Publishing Co.

Word Problems Using Tables - 1

When using a table, read it carefully. Make certain you understand what facts are being presented.

Average Life Span of Animals

Bat - 17 years	Housefly - 2 years
Bullfrog - 12 years	Mouse - 4 years
Butterfly - 6 months	Rabbit - 6 years
Box turtle - 138 years	Spider - 2 years
Camel - 29 years	Squirrel - 5 years
Crocodile - 100 years	Starling - 3 years
Deer - 24 years	Tiger - 24 years
Eagle - 80 years	Whale - 52 years
Elephant - 57 years	Worker ant - 5 years
Goat - 17 years	Zebra - 24 years

Do the four **Word Problem Steps:**
1. Read the problem carefully.
2. Look for possible word clues.
3. Decide what you must do.
4. Solve the problem.

HOUSE FLY 2 years

Work the problems on another sheet of paper. Put your answers on this page.

1. About how many more years does the average tiger live than a goat?

   _____

2. Of the animals listed in the table, which one lives for the shortest time? What is that animal's average life span?

   _____

3. Of the animals listed in the table, which one has the longest average life span? What is that animal's average life span?

   _____

4. What is the difference between the average life span of an elephant and a whale?

   _____

5. Suppose a bullfrog meets with an accident and dies 3 years before it had reached its average life span age? How long would that bullfrog live?

   _____

6. How many of the animals in the table have an average life span of 5 or more years?

   _____

7. By how many years does the average crocodile outlive an average squirrel?

   _____

8. Suppose a mouse were able to live twice as long as the average life span for mice. How old would that mouse be?

   _____

Word Problems Using Tables - II

Read the table carefully. Make certain you understand what facts are being presented. Then use the four **Word Problem Steps** to answer the questions below.

The Sunnyside Rangers Baseball Team		
Player	**Times at Bat**	**Hits**
Anderson, Bunky	50	10
Baranco, Jill	12	3
Fowler, Billy	48	12
Gates, Jerrie	32	8
Holten, Randi	49	15
Larson, Jonny	16	4
O'Brien, Archie	60	18
Rogers, Jose	50	20
Stella, Mimi	36	9
Tessler, Tim	43	17
Waite, Moose	60	12

Work the problems on another sheet of paper. Put your answers on this page.

1. How many more times was Billy Fowler at bat than Mimi Stella? _____

2. How many fewer hits did Jill Baranco get than Archie O'Brien? _____

3. Of the players on the Sunnyside Rangers, how many were at bat more than 16 times? _____

4. Of the players on the Sunnyside Rangers, how many had fewer than 11 hits? _____

5. What percent of the time did Jonny Larson get a hit? _____

6. What was the average number of times Jonny Larson was at bat to get a hit? _____

7. What percent of the time did Moose Waite get a hit? _____

Word Problems Using Graphs - 1

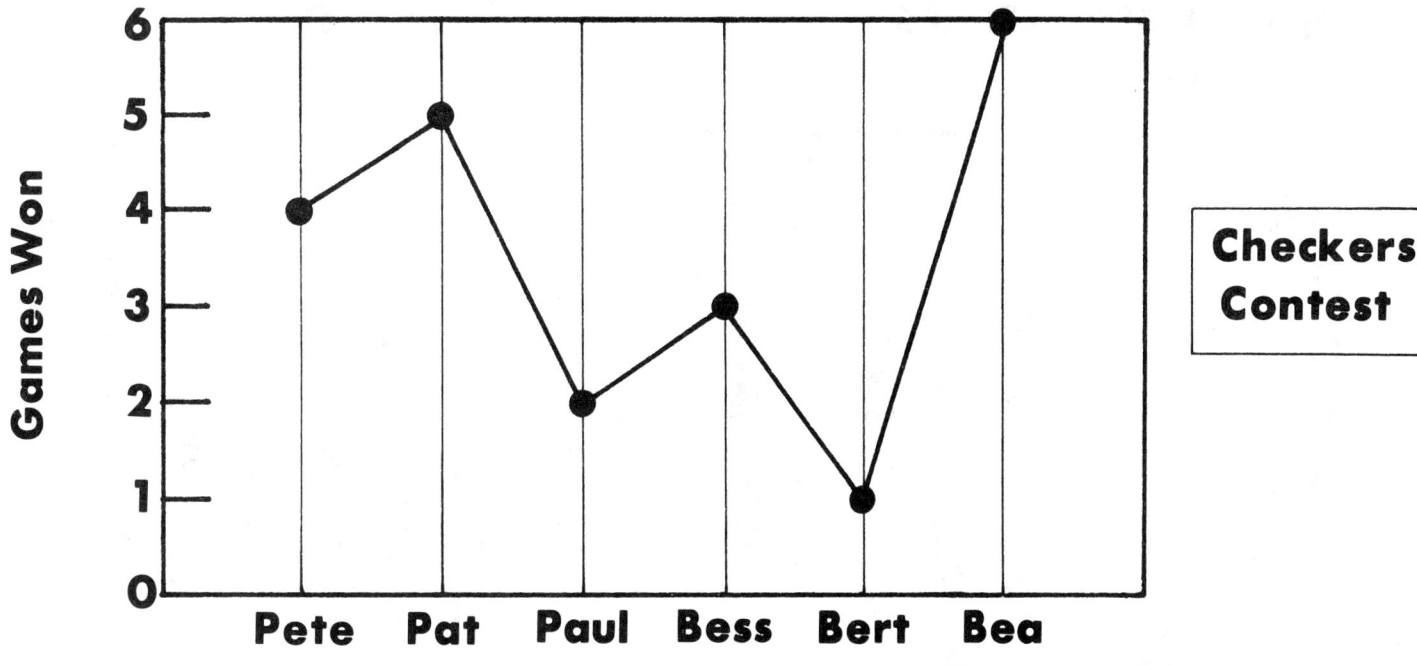

Checkers Contest

1. Six persons played in the checkers contest. Who won the most games?

   _____

2. If Paul had won 3 more games, what would his total number of wins have been?

   _____

3. If you added Pete's wins to those of Bess, how many fewer than 15 wins would the total be?

   _____

4. How many more wins would Bert need to have 1 more win than Bea?

   _____

5. How many fewer games did Paul win than Pat?

   _____

6. If Bess had won 3 more games, how many more games would she have won than Bert?

   _____

7. How many players won more than 2 games?

   _____

Word Problems Using Graphs - II

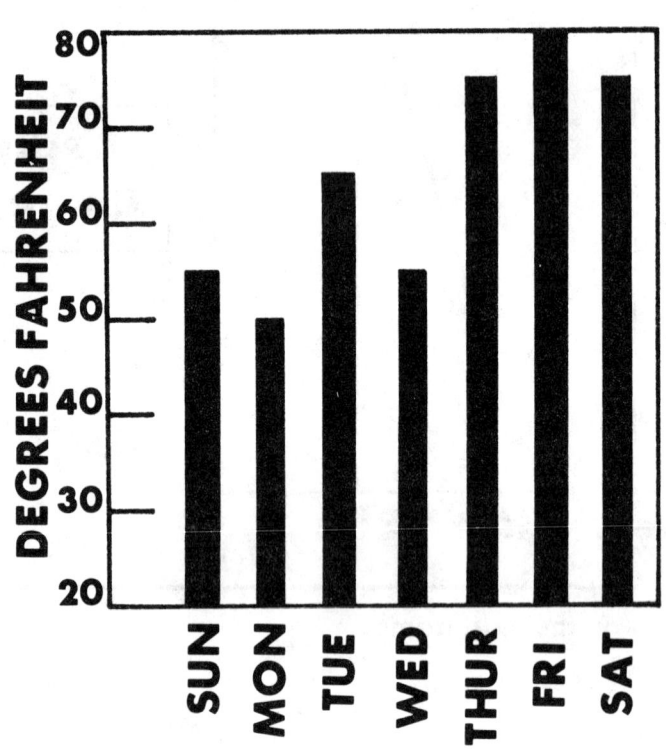

HIGH TEMPERATURES FOR WEEK

GRAPH 1

LOW TEMPERATURES FOR WEEK

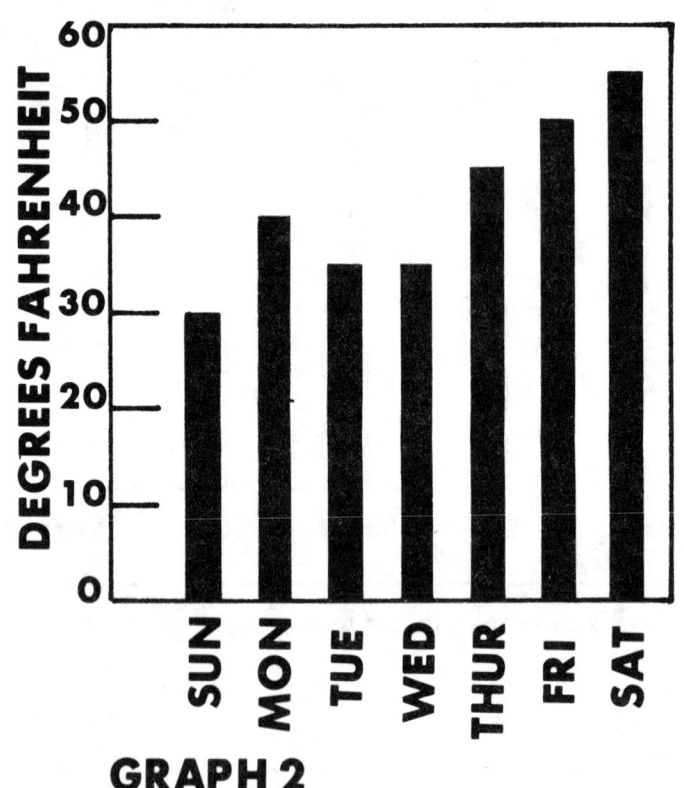

GRAPH 2

1. What is the temperature range on Graph 1? _____

2. What is the temperature range on Graph 2? _____

3. On what day was the highest temperature recorded in the week (shown on Graph 1)? _____

4. On what day was the lowest temperature recorded during the same week? _____

5. How many more degrees warmer was it on Thursday than on Wednesday on Graph 1? _____

6. How many degrees of difference was there between high and low on Saturday during the week? _____

7. On how many days did the temperature drop below 50°F during the week? _____

8. If the temperature had gone up an additional 10°F on Monday, what would the highest temperature have been on that day? _____

9. Suppose the temperature on Monday had been 50% higher on Graph 1. What would the temperature reading then have been? _____

28   More word problems concerning graphs   02042   School Zone Publishing Co.

A Mixture of Word Problems - 1

Remember:

The Steps:
1. Read the problem carefully.
2. Look for possible word clues.
3. Decide what you must do.
4. Solve the problem.

Work the problems on another sheet of paper. Put your answers on this page.

1. There was a sale on record albums at the Music Shop. You could buy any record album at a 20% discount during the sale. If the regular price of an album was $6.80, what was the sale price of that album?

   _____

2. The Music Shop sold lots of record albums during the sale. On Monday 198 were sold. Sales for Tuesday, Wednesday, and Thursday were 216, 117, and 229. Friday sales were 257, and Saturday 343 were sold. How many fewer record albums were sold on Wednesday than were sold on Friday?

   _____

3. Amy has been collecting record albums for 3 years. She has 18 in her collection. Buffy owns no albums, but she will be buying 2 albums next week. Cora has 5 albums of her own, and her brother, Dennis, has 23. How many record albums do the 3 girls own this week?

   _____

4. The Music Shop is open from 9:00 A.M. until 9:00 P.M. and is open 6 days a week. How many hours each week is the Music Shop open?

   _____

5. The Music Shop received a shipment of albums in which 1/8 of the albums were defective. The defective records were returned to the company that made them. If there were 296 albums in the shipment, how many defective records were returned?

   _____

6. The Music Shop now has an area of 3200 square feet. The owners want to enlarge their store. They plan to build an addition that will be 30 feet wide and 50 feet long. What will the area of the addition be?

   _____

A Mixture of Word Problems - II

Remember the **Steps:**
1. Read the problem carefully.
2. Look for possible word clues.
3. Decide what you must do.
4. Solve the problem.

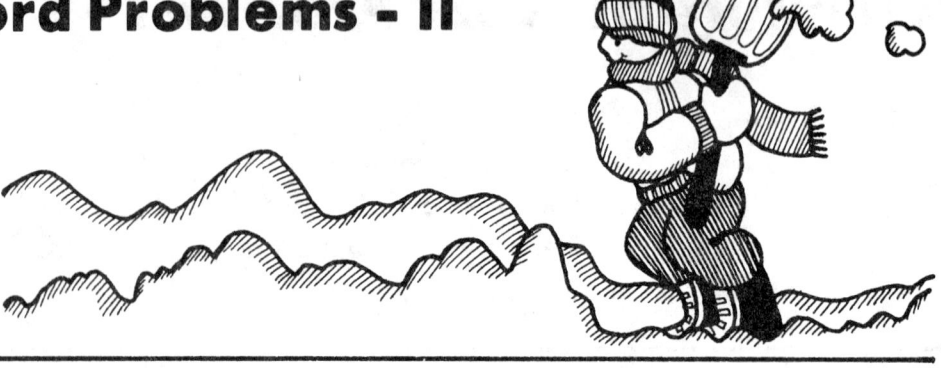

Work the problems on another sheet of paper. Put your answers on this page.

1. Students in Brookwood School had no school on Monday because of snow. On that day snow fell for 10 straight hours. Before the snow ended, 15 inches of snow covered the ground. What was the average number of inches it snowed each hour?

   _____

2. The students who go to Willowdale School never get off because of snow. The temperature is too warm in the part of the country where Willowdale is. In November, 6 inches of rain fell. What was the average rainfall for each day of that month?

   _____

3. One day in February the temperature outside the Willowdale School reached 15°C. On another day that same month the temperature reached 29°C. What was the difference in temperature those 2 days?

   _____

4. There are many sunny days in the Willowdale School area. At least 5 days are sunny each week. How many sunny days could you expect if you went to Willowdale School for 12 weeks?

   _____

5. During one year 24" of snow fell at Brookwood School. The next year the snowfall was 36". What percent of increase was there in snow in this year over that of the previous year?

   _____

6. Students at Brookwood School found that about 40 cm of snow equaled 4 cm of water. If there were 16 cm of water, about how many cm of snow would that equal?

   _____

7. In summer the weather sometimes gets quite hot where the Brookwood School students live, but winters can be very cold. On the 15th of August one year the temperature was 102°F. That was 101° warmer than it was on January 15 of that year. What was the temperature on that day in January?

   _____

Working additional assorted word problems   02042   School Zone Publishing Co.

Page 1
1. 1,241
2. 37
3. 98¢
4. 3,220

Page 2
1. 8
2. 53 cm
3. 426
4. 27,397

Page 3
1. 69
2. 1,221
3. 585
4. 76
5. 344
6. 489
7. 19
8. 87

Page 4
1. 18
2. 2,685
3. 1,470
4. 75

Page 5
1. 270
2. 216
3. 16,380
4. $74,186
5. 936
6. 275
7. 21,600

Page 6
1. 22
2. 54
3. 53
4. 6

Page 7
1. 21
2. 62R11
3. 5,120
4. 43R5
5. 135
6. 11,000

Page 8
1. 336
2. 49
3. $2.00
4. $12.00
5. 4:45
6. 6
7. 287
8. 2

Page 9
1. 21
2. 2083R4
3. 255,000
4. 83
5. 113
6. 98
7. 18

Page 10
1. 148
2. $150
3. $4
4. 30¢
5. 167

Page 11
1. 149
2. 12
3. 7
4. 6
5. 238

Page 12
1. 2
2. 2
3. 2
4. 380
5. 16
6. 27

Page 13
1. 30 3/5 cm
2. 2 1/5 in.
3. 5 5/6 oz.
5. 5/12 lb.
5. 3 lbs.
6. 2 1/8 in.
7. 12 in.

Page 14
1. 7 dozen
2. 10
3. 2
4. 33 1/3
5. 9 pieces
6. 1 7/11

Page 15
1. 9.9 in.
2. 15.2 cm
3. $13.61
4. $3.66
5. 441.764
6. 60.36
7. 309.17

Page 16
1. $1.77
2. 48.951
3. 13.43 lbs.
4. 15¢
5. .111

Page 17
1. $1,015.20
2. 89
3. 317
4. 49
5. 20
6. $1.30
7. 987
8. $115,080.85

Page 18
1. 25%
2. 50%
3. 80%
4. 20%
5. 80%
6. 92%

Page 19
1. 475
2. $6.00
3. 81
4. 629
5. $9.60
6. $12.00

Page 20
1. 1%
2. 189
3. 150,500
4. 12%
5. 40%
6. 72
7. $17.40

Page 21
1. 28
2. 500
3. $7.75
4. $1,550
5. 8%
6. 62 1/2%

Page 22
1. 2,004 yards
2. 8 m
3. 288 cm
4. 9 in
5. 870 mm

Page 23
1. 192 sq. ft.
2. 332.5 sq. cm
3. 2,808 sq. in.
4. 3,825.68 sq. m
5. 13.87 sq. m

Page 24
1. 75,600 cubic cm
2. 36 liters
3. 28,125 cubic cm
4. 28.125 liters
5. 20,680 cubic cm
   20.68 liters

Page 25
1. 7 years
2. butterfly
   6 months
3. box turtle
   138 years
4. 5 years
5. 9 years
6. 15
7. 95 years
8. 8 years

Page 26
1. 12
2. 15
3. 9
4. 5
5. 25%
6. 4
7. 20%

Page 27
1. Bea
2. 5
3. 8
4. 6
5. 3
6. 5
7. 4

Page 28
1. 20°F to 80°F
2. 0°F to 60°F
3. Friday
4. Sunday
5. 20°F
6. 20°F
7. 5
8. 60°F
9. 75°F

Page 20
1. $5.44
2. 140
3. 23
4. 72
5. 37
6. 1500 sq. ft.

Page 30
1. 1.5 in.
2. .2 in.
3. 14°C
4. 60
5. 50%
6. 160 cm
7. 1°F